CW01639436

GUIDE
TO
LAW AND THE FAMILY

DAVID MARSH

EASYWAY GUIDES

Easyway Guides
38 Cromwell Road, London E17 9JN

First Edition 1997

British Library cataloguing in Publication Data. A catalogue record is available for this book from the British Library.

ISBN 1 900694 35 2

Printed by BPC Wheaton Ltd, Exeter.
Cover Design by Straightforward Graphics.

CONTENTS

INTRODUCTION

The area of family law, dealing with marriage, marriage breakdown and the rights of individuals - adults and children - is a very complex area by virtue of the fact that often we are dealing with breakdown of relationships between individuals and the aftermath of the breakdown.

Family law is undergoing a radical change and the 1996 Family Law Act was given Royal Assent in July 1996, an Act which is designed to shake up the law of divorce and associated areas such as property rights. The Act has not yet come into force, at the time of writing, although there are a number of pilot schemes underway designed to test the feasibility of sections of the Act.

It is likely that Part Four of the Act dealing with occupation of the family home and domestic violence, will be introduced in the Autumn of this year and Parts 1, 2 and 3 in 1999. Therefore, it will be a while before we see the divorce provisions outlined in Part Two of this book come into force.

The Act is not a consolidating Act and therefore the provisions contained within are amendments to existing legislation, which will need to be used in conjunction with the 1996 Act. In some cases, significant amendments are made.

The 1996 Act was the culmination of several years of debate concerning the divorce law in force in this country and also the rights of individuals who are not married, but cohabiting. The stages leading up to the Act being given Royal assent were often stormy, as the subject matter elicits a diversity of opinion from right across the spectrum.

In this book, which is an introduction to family law, I will be firstly dealing with the law as it stands, before the various sections of the Family Law Act come into being.

Chapter one deals with the law as it relates to divorce and the ground for divorce. The facts which have to be proved are presented, and the section is illustrated with case law as are all the chapters.

Chapter two deals with the rights of occupation of a family home and the different financial and property orders which can be awarded to the parties on the break-up of a marriage.

Chapter three deals with the rather more complicated area of unmarried partners who, although not divorcing, wish to establish rights of occupation in the home (where one party typically does not have an equity stake) and are seeking a financial or property award.

Chapter four deals with financial provision for children, particularly where the parents are living apart.

Chapter five addresses the area of domestic violence in a home and marriage and explores the range of orders available to those unfortunate enough to be party to such events.

Chapter six deals with the legal relationship between children and adults generally and the upbringing of children.

Chapter seven deals with the law as it concerns the protection of children.

Part two of the book examines the 1996 Family Law Act, the provisions of the Act and what changes to current family law will be effected and when they come into force.

The book is written for both the student of family law and also for those who wish to further their general knowledge of this area.

CHAPTER ONE

DIVORCE - THE LEGAL FRAMEWORK

This chapter will outline the law as it relates to the breakdown of a marriage and the steps towards separation and/or divorce. Divorce is almost always a messy and emotional affair and there are many circumstances and events along the way to obtaining a decree which this book cannot possibly cover.

The aim is to outline the basic law and procedural steps involved and illustrate with case law in order to add emphasis and achieve clarity.

The Ground for Divorce

There is one ground for divorce, that is that the person making an application for a divorce, known as the petitioner, must establish that the marriage has irretrievably broken down. The petitioner must also prove five facts:

a) that the respondent has committed adultery and the petitioner finds it intolerable to live with him/ her.

Section 2 (1) of the Matrimonial Causes Act 1973 states that there can be no decree if the parties have lived with each other for more than six months after the discovery of the alleged adultery.

b) that the respondent has behaved in such a way that the petitioner cannot reasonably be expected to live with him.

When deciding on whether this fact is proved, the court will take into account the characters and personalities of individuals and will attempt objectively to arrive at an interpretation of reasonableness.

One significant case was Livingstone-Stallard v Livingstone-Stallard (H.C 1974). According to the judge in that case, Dunn J. the question that must be answered is:

"Would any right thinking person come to the conclusion that this husband has behaved in such a way that this wife cannot be reasonably expected to live with him, taking into account the whole of the circumstances and the characters and personalities of the parties".

c) that the respondent has deserted the petitioner for a period of at least two years immediately preceding the presentation of the petition

A very small percentage of divorce petitions rely on desertion. There are four conditions that must be fulfilled before a spouse will be found to be in desertion:

i) the parties must be physically living apart
ii) the deserting spouse must have the requisite intention
iii) the separation must not have taken place as a result of an agreement between the parties
iv) the deserting spouse must have had good cause for leaving.
v) that the parties have lived apart for a continuous period of at least two years immediately preceding the presentation of the petition and the respondent consents to a decree being granted

This fact has two aspects: the period of living apart and the respondents consent. "Living apart" can mean living under the same roof and not living as man and wife, in addition to one party leaving the other. One key case here was Le Brocq v. Le Brocq (1964) where a wife excluded her husband from her bedroom by fixing a bolt on the door. The two parties communicated only when necessary. However she cooked his meals and he paid her weekly housekeeping. It was found that although there was a separation of bedrooms there still existed one household and therefore they did not live apart.

e) that the parties have lived apart for a period of at least five years immediately preceding the presentation of the petition.

There are several key differences between this section and d). The first is length of time the parties have to have been apart and the fact that the petitioner does not need the other parties consent. However, under section five of the Matrimonial Homes Act the respondent can file a defence that the resulting divorce would mean grave financial or other hardship to him/her and that it would be wrong on these grounds to resolve the marriage. If the court finds that the petitioner can establish another fact for divorce then this undermines the above defence.

The Court will not grant a divorce unless one of these five facts has been proved. The court can refuse to grant a decree if it is satisfied that the marriage has not broken down. No petition for divorce can be filed unless the parties have been married for one year.

Judicial Separation

Although most whose marriage has broken down will get divorced, there are some who, for various reasons will not wish to terminate the marriage, for example for religious reasons. A judicial separation suits such circumstances and although it does not terminate the marriage it will effectively relieve the petitioner of the responsibility of cohabiting with the other party.

Other people may go for judicial separation because they wish to obtain one of the financial orders which a court has the power to make once a separation is granted. The grounds for judicial separation mirror the five facts for divorce. They fall within section 17(1) of the matrimonial Causes Act.

Nullity. Void and Voidable marriages.

The third type of decree that a court can grant is one of nullity. Such decree declares the marriage to be null and void which is quite different from a termination of marriage. A void marriage is a marriage that was never a marriage at all. A voidable marriage is a valid marriage until annulled by decree. As a result the parties to such a marriage must obtain a decree before they are entitled to behave as single people. There are four grounds for nullity, under section 11 of the M.C.A. They are:

a) that it was never a valid marriage under the Marriage Acts 1949-1986
b) that at the time of the marriage either party was already lawfully married
c) that the parties are not respectively male and female
d) in the case of a polygamous marriage entered into outside England and Wales, that either party was at the time of the marriage domiciled in England and Wales.

The most common ground used is where one of the parties was already married.

Section 12 of the Matrimonial Causes Act details six grounds that are available for declaring a marriage voidable. They are:

a) non-consummation of marriage due to the incapacity of either party
b) non-consummation of marriage due to the wilful refusal of the respondent
c) lack of valid consent to the marriage by either party
d) that either party was suffering from mental disorder
e) that the respondent was suffering from VD in a communicable form at the time of the marriage

f) that the respondent was pregnant by someone other than the petitioner at the time of marriage.

The grounds most petitioners use for annulment of a voidable marriage are those relating to non consummation.

The 1996 Family Law Act

As discussed in the introduction to this book, there are significant reforms underway for the whole process of divorce. These will be discussed in further depth in part two of this book.

CHAPTER TWO

RIGHTS TO OCCUPY A PROPERTY OTHER AWARDS

Awards of property and financial awards.

The Matrimonial Homes Act 1983

When homes are vested in one person, complications can arise during or after a divorce. At common law, even though the home (estate) may be vested in the husband, the wife has the right to occupy it. However, this right could be completely undermined by sale of the estate to a third party. In addition, husbands did not give equal rights to homes vested in the names of their wives. The Matrimonial Homes Act (1983) has sought to rectify this.

Section 1 of the M.H.A. where one spouse (owner) has the right to occupy property that is or was the matrimonial home- and the other has not- the other is given a statutory right of occupation in that property. There is a right not to be evicted from it without leave of the court and the right to resume occupation if the non owner is not in occupation (there has been some attempt to evict, for example).

The spouse will only receive benefit of the Act if she needs it. The rights exist until termination of the marriage. The rights can also be restricted or terminated by an earlier court order under the Matrimonial Homes Act s. 1(2).

The non owning spouse can (should) register a statutory rights of occupation as either a land charge, Class F (for unregistered land), or a notice, for unregistered land. If this is done, then any subsequent purchaser for value will buy subject to the statutory rights of occupation.

The Matrimonial Causes Act 1973 Ancillary to Decree proceedings

The above are orders for the benefit of spouses. By sections 23 and 24 of the Matrimonial Causes Act 1973 the court can grant one or more of the following orders for the benefit of a spouse against another:

a) periodical payments order
b) a secured periodical payments order
c) an order for lump sum or sums
d) a transfer of property order
e) a settlement of property order
f) a variation of settlement order
g) an order extinguishing an interest in a settlement.

None of these orders can be made until a decree of divorce, nullity or judicial separation has been granted. However, a spouse is barred from an order if he or she has remarried prior to the application.

Periodic payments secured and unsecured

This is an order where one spouse should pay another a periodic sum of money. If it is secured this means that it is charged upon a property owned by the spouse. Secured payments can continue beyond the death of a spouse, unsecured payments do not. The court has the power to vary or terminate an order.

Lump sum

This is an order where one spouse pays another a lump sum, either in part or as a lump sum.

Transfer of property

This is an order that one spouse transfers to the other property to which the former is entitled. Property can cover anything from houses and flats, jewellery, vehicles, furniture and so on. The M.C.A does not define property.

Settlement of property order and variation of settlement order

The former is an order that one spouse settle property to which he/she is entitled for the benefit of another. Property is widely interpreted. The variation of a settlement order is an order that any ante- or post nuptial settlement made on the spouse should be varied for their benefit.

By section 25(1) of the M.C.A. it is provided that, when deciding whether and how to exercise its powers, the court must consider all the circumstances of the case, but give first consideration to the welfare of any minor children of the family. In Suter v. Suter and Jones (C.A. 1986) it was held that giving first consideration to the welfare of the children in financial proceedings did not mean that the welfare of the children overrode all other considerations.

The Child Support Act affects the above, however, where child maintenance is calculated using rigid formula under the jurisdiction of the Child Support Agency, discussed further on in this book..

Section 25(2) of the Matrimonial Causes Act directs the court to have regard to the following factors when exercising their powers to make financial provision for a spouse:

a) Income, earning capacity, property and other financial resources.

b) Financial needs, obligations and responsibilities.

c) Standards of living (enjoyed by family prior to breakdown).

d) Age of parties and duration of marriage.

e) Disabilities

f) Contributions to the welfare of the family. It is specifically provided that this includes any contribution made by looking after the home or caring for the family. Thus the wife, who gives up her job and contributes nothing to the family in hard cash, but is the home maker and child rearer, has the value of such activities recognised.

g) Conduct. This is a vague principle and relates to gross misconduct, one party against another.

h) The value of any lost benefit. This could be, for example, pension rights, which parties might lose on a decree being granted.

In addition to the factors listed above, there are other considerations for the courts. By section 25A(1) of the M.C.A. the court is placed under a duty to consider whether it is appropriate to make orders that will terminate the parties financial obligations to each other as soon after the decree as it thinks reasonable. Section 25A(2) creates another obligation on the court. If it has decided that an order for periodical payments must be made (this not ordering a clean break) then it must consider whether to order that the payments must cease after a specified period, a period designed to permit an adjustment to financial independence without undue hardship.

The court has no duty to order a clean break, immediate or delayed; it gives a duty to consider only whether it should order a clean break in every case where it was asked to exercise its financial powers on divorce (or nullity).

Orders for the benefit of children

Children of the family can have the same types of orders made in their favour, against either parties of the marriage, as can the parties themselves. Chapter 4 discusses this in further depth.

Financial awards - The Domestic Proceedings and Magistrates Court Act 1978

It may be the case that one party may want an order against another but cannot or does not wish to issue decree proceedings. The D.P.M.C.A. is one of several statutes that gives the courts power to order financial relief without the necessity of first obtaining an order relating to the status of the marriage itself. Three different situations are covered by the Act.

Sections 1 and 2 of the D.P.M.C.A.

Although the applicant is not seeking any type of decree, he still has to establish one of the following grounds set out in section 2:

a) that the respondent has failed to provide reasonable maintenance for the applicant
b) that the respondent has failed to provide or make proper contribution towards the reasonable maintenance of a child of the family
c) that the respondent has behaved in such a way that the applicant cannot reasonably be expected to live with him
d) that the respondent has deserted the applicant.

There is no definition of the term "reasonable maintenance" in the Act. The court has to take into account the parties respective positions in making their determination. Once the applicant has proved one of the grounds the court has the power to do the following:

a) make an order that the respondent should pay periodical payments to the applicant and/or a child of the family.

b) that the respondent should pay a lump sum to the applicant and/or a child of the family, such lump sum not to exceed £1,000.

Orders for periodic payments cease on the death of the payer. Orders for periodic payments to a spouse cease on remarriage of the spouse. The rules for cessation of payments to children are the same as under the Matrimonial Causes Act. Further orders for periodical payments that are payable to a spouse, either for herself or a child, cease if the parties continue to cohabit or resume cohabitation after the making of the order for a period or periods exceeding six months.

Once a ground is proved, a court has to decide whether to make any order at all. Welfare of children is the usual first consideration.

Financial awards - section 27 of the Matrimonial Causes Act 1973

The courts can grant periodical payments, secured or unsecured, and lump sum for spouses and children of the family on proof simply of failure to provide reasonable maintenance. Again, section 27 provides a means of obtaining orders for financial relief without issuing decree proceedings. However, it is another provision that is little used, despite the fact that the range of orders is wider than under the D.P.M.C.A.

Financial and property awards - section 15 of the Children Act 1989

Section 125 of the Children Act provides for the grant of a range of orders for the benefit of a child. The applicant must be a parent or guardian of the child and the orders can be made against a parent.

Orders depend on parenthood not marriage. The nature of the orders possible under the CA is discussed in chapter 7.

CHAPTER THREE

RIGHTS TO OCCUPY AND OTHER AWARDS

Unmarried partners and spouses who are not divorcing

This chapter relates to spouses who do not seek a decree and to partners who have never been married to each other. In relation to the former, the following rights are important where divorce is not contemplated, or where a spouse has become insolvent or died.

With cohabitees, the Matrimonial Causes Act does not apply, so these are their only rights with regard to joint property. The only difference between the two classes is that cohabitees have to prove to the courts that they had a settled relationship which was intended to be permanent.

Establishing a trust

When dealing with land there will always be documentary evidence as to ownership-the title deeds. It may be that both parties own the land or just one. However, in some cases of joint ownership this is not spelt out. Here there is a presumption that the legal owners are each entitled to an equal share of the beneficial estate. Further, the legal estate in the home may be vested in the sole name of one of the cohabitees. Here, there is a presumption that the beneficial interest also belongs exclusively to that person.

In both these situations consideration of the title deeds alone will not necessarily provide the answer to an ownership dispute. Extrinsic evidence to rebut the presumptions can be deduced by evidence of the existence of a trust behind the deeds.

Trusts are generally categorised as express, implied, resulting and constructive. Express trusts are not common in the family context. The other trusts, or distinctions are of little relevance. What is of relevance is the circumstances in which the court will accept that the trust has arisen, whether resulting, implied or constructive.

Payment towards the purchase price

Where one party provides the whole or the part of the purchase price for property that is conveyed into another persons name, there is a presumption that the first party intended that he should benefit and the second party should hold the property on trust for him, either exclusively or in part, i.e. the beneficial estate "results" in whole or in part, to A. The trust is therefore known as a resulting trust.

The concept of resulting trust is rarely directly applicable in the family context because usually the home is not purchased outright but by way of mortgage.

Two cases in the House of Lords Petit v. Petit (1969) and Gissing V.Gissing (1979) serve to highlight the complicated area of trusts. Both cases concerned a spouse who did not have an interest in the legal estate in the home claiming to be entitled to a beneficial interest by way of trust. There was unanimous decision in both cases that a trust could arise where both parties had intended that it should. The court should look for a common intention that both parties should be beneficially entitled (common intent).

Proof of conduct from which the court can infer the common intent is not sufficient. The woman (in these cases) must also prove that she has acted "to her detriment or significantly altered her position in reliance on the common intent" before a trust in her favour will arise.

Therefore, before such a trust can be established, the courts will scrutinise the parties conduct for two reasons: the first to ascertain that there was the common intent; the second to ascertain that the woman has acted upon it. The crucial questions are then seen to be what sort of conduct will give rise to the inference of common intent and what sort of conduct will show that the woman has acted upon it?

The most recent and authoritative statements on these issues are to be found in the leading judgement of Lord Bridge in Lloyds Bank PLC v. Rosset. Express discussions between the parties as to their interests in the property do not amount to conduct from which a common intent can be inferred. what is looked for are:

" direct contributions to the purchase price by the partner who is not the legal owner, whether initially or by payment of mortgage instalments". These "will readily justify the inference necessary to the creation of a constructive trust. But...it is extremely doubtful whether anything less will do".

An express agreement

Where there is evidence of the parties having entered into"an agreement, arrangement or understanding that the property is to be shared beneficially" then in some circumstances, the court will hold that a trust has arisen. The finding of such an agreement can only be based upon express discussions between the parties.

However, proving an agreement is not the end of the matter. the woman has to show, as before, that she has acted to her detriment or significantly altered her position in reliance on the agreement before the court will hold that a trust in her favour has arisen.

Two points need to be made in relation to this type of trust. First, it can be distinguished from an express trust, which does not require an agreement between the parties, nor the woman having acted to her detriment. Second, it can be distinguished from a trust arising from the common intention of the parties, because the court does not infer an agreement. Direct evidence of it must be present.

Again, the crucial issue is the sort of conduct that will be required before, for this type of trust, the woman will be held to have acted to her detriment.

Quantification of beneficial interests under a trust

In the past few years, there have been a number of cases concerning the quantification of shares. Where the cases concern a resulting trust, the shares are determined in relation to each parties contribution. Where the case concerns a trust arising from an express agreement of the parties or a trust arising from their common intent, as inferred from their conduct, the shares are determined by reference to that agreement or, if there is none, their common intent. Where there is no common agreement, the court is entitled to look at:

"all the circumstances surrounding the acquisition of the property, things said and done then and subsequently" including "their respective financial contributions to the purchase price. B v B (H.C. 1988)

"the contributions which in total each had made. Those contributions would include, in addition to the original contribution, sums contributed to discharge of the ... mortgage and the cost of capital improvements. (Passee v. Passee (C.A. 1988).

Proprietary Estoppel

Estoppel is the principle that prevents a person from exercising or asserting his legal rights and usually the principle can only be pleaded in defence of an action to exercise or assert those rights. Proprietary estoppel, however, can only be used to assert contrary rights. The circumstances in which such a situation will be recognised by law are rigorously defined.

In Coombes v. Smith (H.C. 1987) the court stated that a claim to a share in the beneficial interest of a property based upon proprietary estoppel would only succeed if the claimant can show:

a) that she had made a mistake as to her legal rights in the property
b) that she had spent money or done some other legal act as a result of that mistake
c) that the defendant knew of his own rights in the property inconsistent with those she had
d) that he knew of her mistaken belief
e) that he encouraged her to act as above.

Occupation of the home

If a woman is successful in establishing that she has a beneficial interest in the property, she may then be faced with a demand that nevertheless the property be sold so that the man may at least realise his share. This could equally happen to a woman who is a joint owner on the face of the deeds. An immediate sale of the home, however, can cause hardship.

By the Law of Property Act s30 the court can order the sale of the property subject to a trust for sale. But it can also refuse to make such an order. Generally it will do so if it is satisfied that the purpose of the trust is still unfulfilled. Thus if the home was in reality bought as a home for the family, it is likely that any application for the sale of the home prior to the children reaching majority age will be refused, despite the breakdown of marriage. Thus there is protection for the woman to some extent.

Because of the facts of their relationship the woman may not be able to establish that they each own a share of the property. As a last resort, such a woman may be at least able to establish a right to occupy a home after the relationship has broken down.

This may be possible if the circumstances show that the man has granted her a licence to stay on his property, a licence that was given for consideration and cannot be revoked by giving notice but only in accordance with the contract. Courts are often asked to infer the granting of such licences. In Tanner v. Tanner (C.A. 1975) because the woman gave up a protected tenancy to go and live with the man and their children at his house, the court inferred the grant of a licence to occupy until his children left school. However, in Coombes v. Smith the court rejected the alternative claim of the plaintiff for a licence for the duration of her life. The inference of a licence like this is based on the facts of each case and can be an extremely artificial exercise.

CHAPTER FOUR

PROVIDING FOR CHILDREN

In July 1990, the Government announced the setting up of the Child Support Agency, brought into being by the Child Support Act 1991. The purpose of the agency was to improve on the then existing child maintenance system which, according to the government allowed errant fathers to avoid maintenance with no real sanctions. The Government stated:

"The present system is unnecessarily fragmented, uncertain in its results, slow and ineffective. It is largely based on discretion. The cumulative effect is uncertainty and inconsistent decisions about how much maintenance should be paid".

The C.S.A came into force on April 5th 1993. The agency is responsible for all new cases, cases where the claimant is on income support and family credit. By April 1997, alphabetically , all cases will fall under the remit of the agency.

The principle of the C.S.A. is that whatever the changes in parents relationships, they cannot change their responsibility towards their children. There is a formula laid out which fixes maintenance levels and Child Support Officers have wide powers to collect information.

The C.S.A applies to a "qualifying Child" defined by section 3(1) of the Act as a child where one or both of his parents is an "absent" parent. This means a parent who is not living in the same household as the child, notwithstanding contact arrangements.

The C.S.A applies only to natural or adoptive parents or persons treated as parents under the H.F.E.A. The absent parent is required to make periodical payments in accordance with fixed criteria.

The C.S.A. lays down a maintenance requirement, the amount needed to maintain the child based on income support criteria. There is a maintenance assessment which is the assessable income of the absent parent, adding the income of person with care and dividing by two.

There is also an additional element whereby the absent parent can be called upon to contribute further up to a statutory maximum. There is also a protected income level which is designed to ensure that the absent parent is better off than he would be on income support.

Once the assessment is made, the Agency may carry out collections and enforcement and will automatically do so where the claimant is on income support.

The Agency may make deductions from earnings orders under s 31, and may apply to the Magistrates for a liability order under s 33, and in the event of wilful refusal or culpable neglect, imprisonment for up to six weeks under section 40.

S 9(1) states that no agreement for maintenance can prevent a person with care from applying for an assessment and any clause purporting to exclude that right is void.

The maintenance assessment can only be made on application to the agency, but in respect of persons with care on benefit, they must authorise action on penalty of a reduction in benefit under section 46(5) of 20% for six weeks followed by 10% for a further year. Under s6(2) the requirement to co-operate may be waived if an officer is satisfied that there is a risk to a claimant or any child of, suffering harm or distress.

Maintenance assessments and special cases Regulations 1992 give relief to an absent parent who has regular contact with his child. The assessment is reduced if the child spends 104 nights or more each year with the absent parents.

The C.S.A has had a stormy ride since it came into being and there are claims that there is a lack of flexibility in the calculation, absence of appeals and disregard for previous arrangements. There are also claims that it is not effective as it should be.

Although the C.S.A. supplants the courts powers, the sections of the Matrimonial Causes Act 1973 and Children's Act 1989 are not repealed and the provisions are still relevant. Courts have a role in the following circumstances:

a) Where the absent parent is sufficiently wealthy to be able to top up the maximum maintenance under the C.S.A.

b) Where the child is receiving full time instruction or training requiring provision of some or all of the expenses, e.g. school fees.

c) Where the child is disabled, orders may be made to meet some or all of the expenses attributable to that disability.

d) Where 17 and 18 year olds are not in full time education.

e) Where there is a lump sum or transfer of property order.

f) Where the child is a "child of the family" and not a qualifying child.

Matrimonial Causes Act 1973

Within the framework of the above children can have the same types of orders made in their favour, against either of the parties to the marriage as can the parties themselves. The order can direct payment to the child or third party. Generally, no application for an order in favour of a child over 18 can be made. Periodical payments orders secured or unsecured must terminate when the child reaches 17 unless the court decides to the contrary. Both types of payments must cease on the death of the payer.

Matters taken into account when making an order

As with spouse orders, the first consideration of the court, when deciding whether and how to exercise it powers, is the welfare of any minor children of the family.

The courts, under M.C.A. s 25(3) will have regard to:

a) the financial needs of the child

b) the income, earning capacity, property and other financial resources of the child

c) any physical or mental disability of the child

d) the type of education or training he was receiving or was expected to receive by the parties to the marriage

e) the financial assets and needs of the parties, the standard of living enjoyed by the family prior to the breakdown of the marriage and any physical or mental disability of the parties.

The M.C.A. s 25(4) provides further factors to be taken into account when the court is considering making an order against a party to the marriage who is not a parent of the child, and include, for example the liability of any other person to maintain the child.

The Children Act 1989, Section 15

Section 15 of the CA provides for the grant of a range of financial and property awards for children subject to the C.S.A. The applicant must be the parent or guardian of the child and orders can be made against the parent.

It must be remembered that the availability of these orders is not dependent upon the parties being married to each other, it is dependent upon parenthood. However, married parents may make use of section 15 where there is no pending divorce proceedings.

The court has the power to make the following orders:

a) that either parent pay periodical payments for the benefit of the child, secured or unsecured

b) that either parent pay a lump sum for the benefit of the child

c) that either parent transfer property to which he is entitled to the child

d) that either parent do settle such property for the benefit of the child.

All the above orders benefit children alone. Orders for unsecured periodical payments cease on the death of the payer and for both types of periodical payments the rules for cessation when the child reaches a specific age apply.

The CA schedule one lists the matters that the court must take into account when deciding what order to make. They bear some similarity to those listed in the M.C.A. s 25(3), the factors relevant for child orders ancillary to decree proceedings.

CHAPTER FIVE

DOMESTIC VIOLENCE

Violence in the family is a common occurrence and can cause a great deal of misery to the victim of that violence. Although violence is not just physical but mental too, it is an unfortunate fact that much of the incidence of domestic violence is by men against women.

Physical violence is a criminal offence. However, the criminal law is concerned primarily with punishment and does not take any steps to protect the victim. This section is mainly concerned with civil remedies, mainly the injunction. An injunction can be granted to restrain violence and also molestation.

Horner v. Horner (1983) defined molestation as "any conduct which can properly be regarded a such a degree of harassment as to call for the intervention of the court". There are cases where an injunction restraining such behaviour will not be sufficient protection. In these case there can be no real alternative but to make an order separating the parties, an order which ousts one of them from the home.

These orders, ouster orders have many variations, for example, to prevent one party using certain rooms in the house or an ouster from the house or even the area.

Most commonly the woman seeks an order against the man. The powers can equally be used by man against woman.

Inherent Jurisdiction

By section 37(1) of the Supreme Courts Act 1981, the High Court is given the power to grant injunctions "in all cases in which it appears to be just and convenient to do so". This power is also given to the county court by section 38 of the County Courts Act 1984.

In the family law sphere, this power is frequently used to grant non-molestation injunctions as a part of a divorce suit. An injunction under these Acts can only be granted in support of a legal or equitable right. It is accepted that everyone has a right not to be subjected to assault and battery and this has been relied upon by the courts, expressly or impliedly, when granting a wife a non-molestation injunction against her violent husband, as part of divorce proceedings. It is possible, however, that such injunctions are too wide.

In the case Patel v. Patel (1988) an injunction restraining the respondent from "assaulting, molesting or otherwise interfering or communicating with the applicant" had been granted to an unmarried woman as part of an action alleging trespass to the person. It was redrawn by the court to restrain assault and molestation only. This was ordered on the basis that there is no right not to be harassed that could be supported by the words "otherwise interfering or communicating with".

Ouster injunctions present a different problem. In practice, they may still be dealt with as part of the divorce proceedings but the Court must apply the principles of the M.H.A. in arriving at their decision.

There have been conflicting decisions in the court of appeal concerning the power to grant ouster orders in proceedings concerning children.

In Ashbury v. Millington (1986) the court said it had no powers under the guardianship of Minors Act 1971, nor was there the power under the inherent jurisdiction. This was affirmed by F(minors) (Parental Home: Ouster) (1993) where a mother argued that her father should be excluded from the house so that she could live there with the children. She relied on the inherent jurisdiction and in the alternative, a CA, section 8 specific issue order. Her appeal was dismissed. An injunction under the inherent jurisdiction was not available and section 8 orders could not affect the fathers right of occupation.

Finally, the injunction must bear a sensible relationship to the proceedings in which it is sought.

Richards v. Richards (1983)

A principle was established in the above case which set an important limitation on the powers of the court under the Supreme Courts Act. In this case, the court decided that the power could not be used to regulate the occupation of the matrimonial home because Parliament had enacted a statute specifically designed to cover this problem, the Matrimonial Homes Act 1967 (now 1983). It was not open to the litigants to avoid the detailed provisions of an Act designed to meet a specific problem by calling on an earlier and more general power. Many ouster orders (which in effect regulate the occupation of the matrimonial home) had been made under the general power contained in the S.C.A. s 37(1), between the operational date of the Matrimonial Homes Act 1967 and the delivery of the judgements in Richards v. Richards and their jurisdictional basis was thus undermined.

The Matrimonial Homes Act 1983

Given the above, it is necessary to consider the provisions contained within this Act. Where at least one spouse has right of occupation in a dwelling that at one time has been the matrimonial home the court has the power to make an order:

a) restricting or terminating those rights

b) prohibiting, suspending or restricting the exercise of those rights

c) requiring either spouse to permit the exercise by the other of those rights.

A right of occupation can be created in many ways. One or both of the parties may own the property. Such a right can be created by contract, tenancy or licence. A spouse may have the statutory rights of occupation themselves created by the M.H.A.

The powers of the courts under the M.H.A. do have limitations. First, it would not seem possible to oust a spouse from an area around the matrimonial home. Secondly, there is no power to grant non molestation injunctions under the M.H.A. Thirdly, the M.H.A. only applies to married partners.

Exercise of the powers of the court

The M.H.A. spells out the principles to be applied in the grant of ouster injunctions. By s 1(3) of the M.H.A., the court may make such an order regulating the occupation of the matrimonial home " as it thinks just and reasonable having regard to:

a) the conduct of the spouses in relation to each other

b) their respective needs and financial resources
c) the needs of any children

d) all the circumstances of the case.

In Richards v. Richards, it was decided that none of the factors listed in M.H.A. s 1 (3) including the needs of children, was to be accorded a priority over others. This is in striking contrast to the principle contained in the Childrens Act s 1(1) which states that when a court decides any question with respect to the upbringing of a child, the child's welfare shall be the courts paramount consideration.

Such order as is just and reasonable

Apart from the factors specifically mentioned in the M.H.A. s 1(3) the court is enjoined to make such an order as is "just and reasonable". In a number of recent cases, the Court of Appeal has reminded lower courts that they must also take into account the draconian nature of an ouster order. As was stated in Wiseman v.Simpson (1988):

"To order any man or woman to leave his or her home is a drastic thing to do. The importance of a home is to be measured not only by the strength of the tie created by time to one particular place but also by the difficulty in getting another".

The facts of their case were that there was no recent history of violence between the parties but there was a very tense atmosphere in the home caused by there frequent quarrels. the man had refused to give the woman any housekeeping money and the woman had refused to do any housekeeping. Eventually she had locked him out. In resisting his application for re-entry, the woman alleged that the situation was retarding the development of their 18 month old child. Evidence was also given that the only other accommodation available to her was sharing a room in her parents house and that, if she and her partner remained in the same home, she could not claim state benefits for her support.

In rescinding the grant of the ouster order and remitting the case back to the county court for a rehearing, the Court of Appeal stated that, although the judge had taken account of all the factors listed in the M.H.A. s 1(3) the drastic nature of the ouster order had not been considered. Further, the court clearly felt that the evidence of damage to the child was very weak.

The Domestic Violence and Matrimonial Proceedings Act 1976

By Section 1 of the D.V.A. a spouse may apply for one or more of the four types of injunctions:

a) a non-molestation injunction relating to the applicant

b) a non-molestation injunction relating to any child living with the applicant

c) an ouster injunction, relating to the matrimonial home, a part of it or area around it

d) an injunction requiring the other spouse to permit the applicant to enter and remain in the home or a part of it. Although the Act puts no limit on the duration of any orders granted under it, it is seen as an emergency measure and, in practice, the court will consider putting time limits on most ouster injunctions. Three months is seen as appropriate.

The extension of the courts powers under the D.V.A. to co-habitees has been problematic. There was an attempt to limit the grant of injunctions to cases where there was a legal right that needed the power of the injunction. This argument was not successful. In Davis v. Johnson, the Lords rejected this argument. Therefore, co-habitees have the right to obtain ouster injunctions also.

The Exercise of the courts powers

Before it will grant a non molestation injunction the court must be satisfied that there has been some form of molestation, and also that there is a need for an order preventing a repetition of the behaviour.

The Domestic Proceedings and Magistrates Courts Act 1978

By section 16 of the D.P.M.C.A. a spouse may apply to a magistrates court for either or both of two types of orders:

a) an order that the other spouse should not use or threaten to use violence against the applicant or a child of the family (a personal protection order)

b) an order that the other spouse should leave and/or not enter the matrimonial home (an exclusion order) and, if appropriate, should permit the applicant to enter and remain in the matrimonial home.

The magistrates court has no power to restrain molestation that does not involve violence or the threat of it. Further, the magistrates court has no power to grant relief to an unmarried partner. Nor does it have the power to exclude from an area around the home.

To obtain an order forbidding the use of threats of violence, the applicant must prove that violence is real, or the threat of it. To obtain the order excluding the respondent from the home, the applicant must prove that she or a child of the family is in danger of physical injury.

Enforcement

It is often difficult enforcing injunctions. In many cases it is hard enough obtaining the injunction. Enforcing is another matter. Applicants have to rely upon the courts powers to punish respondents for disobedience and hope that this, or the threat of it will, indirectly, force respondents to obey such orders in the future. Breach of an injunction is contempt and is punishable by a fine or imprisonment. Strictly however, breach of an order made by a magistrates court is not contempt. However, s 63 of the Magistrates Court Act 1980 allows it to levy fines or order imprisonment.

The applicant must begin proceedings for punishment in the event of breaching an injunction. There are disadvantages, in terms of stress and cost and, to avoid these disadvantages, a power of arrest can be attached to injunctions and orders. The exercise of power of arrest has immediate and dire consequences. Therefore, its grant is hedged about by limitations.

Under the D.V.A. the court has to be satisfied that the respondent has caused actual bodily harm to the applicant or a child living with her and is likely to repeat this. However, the power to attach a power of arrest to an injunction is not limited to injunctions granted under the D.V.A. itself: it is available "when, on the application of a spouse, a court grants an injunction" of the relevant type. Thus, a power of arrest has also been attached to such injunctions granted under the general powers of the Supreme Courts Act. section 37.

Orders granted under the D.P.M.C.A. are not covered by the D.V.A. s 2 but by the D.P.M.C.A. s 18. Again, however, only some of the orders that can be granted under the D.P.M.C.A. s 16 can have the power of arrest attached to them; those forbidding the use of violence against the applicant or a child of the family by the respondent and those forbidding the entry of the home by the respondent. Again, the court must be satisfied that stringent conditions exist before it can attach a power of arrest, that the applicant or a child of the family has been physically injured by the respondent and that it is likely to happen again.

CHAPTER SIX

CHILDREN AND ADULTS

The relationship between the child and the adult

At birth, the law defines a relationship between a child and his/her parent and no other adults. For many children, the law plays no further part in their upbringing. However, for others events result in the need for additional principles.

The starting point is, however, the relationship between a child and parents. Occasionally, the issue of exactly who is a parent arises.

Medical advances in assisted reproduction have caused problems which resulted in the passing of the Human Fertilisation and Embryology Act 1990, which took effect on August 1st 1991 but relates only to births after that date. There are various types of assisted reproduction, including artificial insemination, in vitro fertilisation (test tube) but as either the sperm or the embryo (or both) may be donated by strangers, it means that a child may not be genetically related to its parents.

The H.F.E.A. s 27(1) provides "where a married woman is carrying or has carried a child as a result of placing in her embryo, sperm or eggs... she is the mother of the child.

As far as the male is concerned, the rule is that the genetic father (the donor of the sperm) is the legal father. However, there are two important exceptions to this rule. First, by s 28 (2) " Where a married woman is expecting a child...notwithstanding that the sperm was not donated by the husband, he and no other person is treated as the father of the child". This section only applies if the husband consented to the wife's treatment. Second, by section 28(3) if donated sperm is used in the course of "licensed treatment" (i.e. licensed under H.F.E.A.) provided for a woman and a man together, then the man is treated as the father of the child. This section clearly covers the co-habitant of the woman.

The H.F.E.A. also deals with surrogacy, where another woman carries the child for a married couple following fertilisation. It should be noted that the Act does not apply where the surrogate is impregnated by sexual intercourse with the husband. Under s 30, the court is empowered to make an order that the child is to be treated as a child of the parties to the marriage, but the following conditions must be satisfied:

1. the parties must be married to each other and be over 18 years of age

2. the order must be within six months of the birth

3. the court must be satisfied that the surrogate mother and the genetic father fully understand and consent to the order

4. the courts must also be satisfied that no money changed hands in connection with the arrangements but reasonable expenses are allowed (clothes, travel etc.).

Paternity disputes

Unless paternity is admitted it must be proved. Such an issue could arise within a number of different types of proceedings and the courts will often need to determine the paternity of the child as a preliminary matter.

The question of paternity can also be dealt with as an issue in its own right. Under the Family Law Act 1986, a person can apply to the court simply for a declaration that a named person is the father.

Paternity can be established in a number of different ways, for example evidence may be adduced of out of court admission by the man; of the fact that the man is registered as the father in the Register of Births Deaths and Marriages; of the man having had sexual intercourse with the mother at the time that conception must have taken place.

Conclusions drawn from the results of blood tests have also been given as evidence. The advent of DNA fingerprinting has strengthened this method. This can be used on any type of human tissue and can provide virtually conclusive proof of paternity. It is only of use if all parties, mother, child and alleged father are tested. The Family Law Reform Act 1969 provides that, where parentage is an issue, the court may order that a person or party to the proceedings submit to a blood test.

Status of children

The legal effect of the physical relationship between parent and child is sometimes dependent upon whether the child was born to married or unmarried parents. At common law, a child born to unmarried parents had no rights against his father and remoter ancestors and, to begin with, no rights even against his mother Changes in the law have eroded that position. Amendments in the legal position of the child born to unmarried parents have been affected by either extending the categories of children who were to be taken as having been born to married parents or by specifically providing that those born to unmarried parents should have some of the same rights as those born to married parents. Nevertheless, prior to the FLRA there still existed some significant differences in the legal positions of the two categories of children. The Act was designed to eradicate those differences as much as was thought reasonable. It was also designed to discourage the practice of labelling children as legitimate or illegitimate, which is accepted as negative terminology.

Parental responsibility

Parental responsibility is a new concept introduced by the Children's Act. It is the legal definition of the relationship between parent and child. Parental responsibility is defined by s 3 as:

" all the rights and duties, powers and responsibilities and authority which by law a parent of a child has in relation to the child and his property".

At the birth of the child, the position is that the parental responsibility for a child born to married parents belongs to both parents, the parental responsibility for a child born to unmarried parents belongs exclusively to the mother.

The Law Commission did, however, feel that some provision for the sharing of responsibility between unmarried parents should be made. Accordingly, section 4 of the Children's Act provides that it is possible for two parents to agree parental responsibility. This must be in writing, on a prescribed form and recorded in the principal registry of the family division. Alternatively the father can apply to the court for an order to gain responsibility for sharing.

Parental responsibility can also be gained by non parents. Guardians can be vested with responsibility by parents or a court can make orders granting responsibility, such as an adoption order or a care order.

Although it is impossible for a person to surrender parental responsibility the exercise can be delegated to another, a third party. s 2(9).

For parents married when their child was born and an unmarried mother, parental responsibility can only be terminated by the grant of an adoption order in favour of someone else. This applies also to others who have acquired parental responsibility.

Parental responsibility is owed to a child, defined in the Children's Act, as a person under 18 (save for certain aspects of financial responsibility).

A decision in Gillick v. West Norfolk Health Authority and Another, was quite important in defining this area. In this case the Area Health Authority issued guidelines to doctors practising in the area that it would be lawful to provide contraceptive advice to a person under 16 without consent or knowledge of the child's parents. This was challenged by the plaintiff stating that advice or treatment was an infringement of parental rights. The House of Lords (Lord Scarman et al) thought differently who stated:

" Parental rights yield to the right of the child to make his own decision when he reaches sufficient understanding and intelligence to be capable of making up his own mind on the matter"

The case concerned the then parental right to consent to medical treatment, more specifically contraceptive treatment. Thus it was argued that all parental rights ceased as and when the child had the capacity to make the decision himself.

The Court of Appeal however has taken a dim, somewhat narrow view of the case. Several decisions have served to cloud the waters and again make the issue unclear.

Exercise of parental responsibility

Section 2(7) provides that where parental responsibility is shared, each person having parental responsibility can act alone. An order made under the Children's Act can undermine this, however, such as a residence order. In addition, it may be impossible in practice for one person with parental responsibility to exercise it without the co-operation of the other. For example a married but separated partner may find it impossible to exercise full responsibility without the full co-operation of the other.

Definition of children of the Family

By section 105 of the Children Act, the term "a child of the family", in relation to the parties to a marriage means:

a) a child of both parties

b) any other child, not being a child who is placed with the parties as foster parents...who has been treated by both parties as a child of the family.

The adults (married) need not be the child's natural parents. The relationship is of significance in that financial awards can be made against the adults in favour of a child.

The relationship does not automatically result in the adults having parental responsibility towards the child. This depends on other factors, such as parenthood.

Where it is necessary to prove that a child has been treated as a child of the family the issue is a question of fact to be viewed objectively. But there must be a family in existence before a child can be so treated.

In one case, A v. A (1974), prior to the marriage, the wife falsely told the husband that the child she was carrying was his. They married, but parted before the child's birth. It was held that the child was not the child of the family.

Determination of disputes by the courts

By section 1(5) the court will not to make any order at all under the Children Act unless it considers that by doing so the child would be better off than if no order was made at all.

This is a relatively new principle, introduced by the Children's Act. It had been shown previously that the granting of court orders relating to the upbringing of the children sometimes made the child's position worse rather than better.

When determining any question relating to a child's upbringing or the administration of his property or income, the child's welfare is the courts paramount consideration. This is known as the paramountcy principle.

In Birmingham City Council v. H (A Minor) (1993) the local authority had taken into care a child, aged two, whose mother, aged sixteen, was also in care, and proposed to terminate contract, contrary to the wishes of the mother. The House of Lords held unanimously that the child's welfare was paramount and for the purposes of these proceedings the mother was to be treated as the parent, not as another child who was also subject to the welfare principle.

While of great importance, the principle contained in section 1(1) of the Children Act is very wide. For more specific guidance the courts have to take into account the statutory list of guidelines contained in section 1(3):

a) the ascertainable wishes and feelings of the child (considered in the light of his age and understanding). If at all these should be ascertained by a welfare officer who had been ordered to prepare a report for the court

b) the child's physical, emotional and educational needs

c) the likely effect on the child of any effect in his circumstances

d) the child's age, sex, background and any characteristics of his which the court considers relevant

e) any harm the child has suffered or is at risk of suffering

f) how capable each of his parents or guardians is in meeting his needs

g) the range of powers available to the court under the Children's Act in the proceedings in question.

The courts must also, by section 1(2) take into account the effects of any delay which might be harmful to the child.

The rights of the child

There has been a clear shift from the notion of parental rights over a child to that of parental responsibility. Having said this the law still does not regard the child as an individual who has the same rights as an adult in determining his future. The Children's Act, though, contains a number of provisions that acknowledge the role of children in their own lives. A child may apply for an order under the Act which applies to himself or may refuse to submit to a medical examination directed by the court, when granting an emergency protection order.

CHAPTER SEVEN

DISPUTES
WHEN RAISING CHILDREN

Before the advent of the Children's Act, the law was very complex indeed. All previous orders have been replaced by the provisions of the Children's Act which has simplified matters somewhat.

A new guardianship scheme has been created by the Children's Act (ss 5 and 6) and a new parental responsibility order for unmarried fathers. There are four new orders created by s 8 of the Children's Act, Section 8 Orders:

Residence Order

Contact Order

A Prohibited Steps Order

A Specific Issues Order

Residence order

This is an order which settles the arrangements to be made as to the person with whom the child is to live. It can be made in favour of any person,. with the exception of the local authority. It can be made in favour of more than one person specifying periods of time spent with individuals if they do not live together.

In many cases, the person with parental responsibility will be granted the order. However, it is the person to whom the order is granted who assumes responsibility.

Contact Order

This is an order requiring the person with whom the child resides to allow the child to visit or stay with another person. Again, local authorities are excluded.

Prohibited Steps Order

This is an order directing a person named in the order not to take any specified step in relation to the child without the permission of the court.

Specific Issues Order

This is an order that determines a specific question in connection with any aspect of parental responsibility. An example may mean schools attended, religion etc.

Section 8 orders can be made subject to directions as to their implementation and conditions that must be complied with. None of these orders can be made once a child has reached his 16th birthday or extend beyond then unless there are exceptional circumstances (s9(6) and (7).

Different types of proceedings

The only way for private individuals to take steps to resolve disputes concerning bringing up a child is for one of them to issue proceeding under the Children's Act. Like the above orders, the Children's Act has greatly simplified dispute resolution. The only exceptions to this relate to wardship and adoption.

Under the Children's Act it is possible to apply for an order appointing a guardian of the child (s 5). An order of this type gives parental responsibility. It is also possible for an unmarried father to apply for an order which gives him parental responsibility. The main type of application possible under the Children Act however, is a section 8 order.

An application for such an order can be made in several ways, either as a "free standing application" or as part of "family proceedings" Section 8 defines "family proceedings" The list includes jurisdictions which used to have their own powers to grant orders relating to upbringing of children, for example the M.C.A. It also includes applications under Part One of the Children's Act itself. It should be noted that once family proceedings have commenced, the court can make a section 8 order itself, of its own motion.

Types of applicant

In most cases, it is the parents of the child who are in dispute about its upbringing. However, others with an interest in the child's welfare may also make an application. The Children Act recognises the need for persons other than parents of a child to be able to get orders which relate to the child's upbringing:

Those entitled to apply for any s 8 order:

A parent or guardian of the child

A person who has been granted a residence order

Those entitled to apply for a residence or contact order:

A spouse or ex spouse in relation to whom the child is a child of the family

A person with whom the child has lived for at least three years. This need not be continuous as long as the period does not begin more than five years, nor end more than three months before, the making of the application.

A person who has the consent of the person in whose favour there is a residence order, if one has been granted, the local authority if the child is in care and in any other case any other person with parental responsibility.

The factors a court must take into account when considering making an order are designed to prevent applications deemed not to be serious and also possibly injurious to the child's future well-being.. They include the nature of the persons connection with a child (s 10) (9).

CHAPTER EIGHT

PROTECTION OF CHILDREN

Types of orders available

As in Chapter Seven, before the Children's Act came into being, there were many types of orders available to local authorities which enabled them to offer some form of protection to children. Local authorities could, on passing a specific resolution, assume the role of parent.

The Children's Act makes an attempt to get rid of the uncertainty of the old laws. It replaced all the old laws with a new scheme. In addition, local authorities can no longer pass a parental rights resolution. No child may be taken into care without a court order.

The following orders are available:

Care orders (s 31)

Supervision orders (s 31)

The education supervision order (s 36)

The emergency protection order (s 44)

The child assessment order (s 43).

Care orders

This is an order that commits a child into the care of a local authority. It cannot be made in favour of anyone else. The effect of a care order is that the child in question goes to live in a local authority community home, or with local authority foster parents. The legal effect is that the local authority gains parental responsibility for the child while the order is in force. A care order automatically brings to an end any residence order that exists. But if a parent or guardian has parental responsibility at the time that a care order comes into force, this continues. A care order cannot be made in respect of a child who has reached 17 (16 if married). It lasts until the age of 18.

Supervision orders

This is an order placing the child under the supervision of a local authority or probation officer. This order does not carry any parental responsibility and there is no power to take a child from his home. A supervision order can have conditions attached to it as the court sees fit. A supervision order cannot be made in respect of a child who has reached the age of 17 (16 if married)

Generally, a supervision order has a life span of one year but can be extended to two years.

Education supervision orders

This is an order placing a child under the supervision of the local education authority.

Emergency protection orders

Orders usually take time to activate. For those children requiring emergency protection the above order is issued. It is an order that empowers the local authority or NSPCC to remove a child from its home and also gives the local authority parental responsibility. Applications can be made ex parte, without the necessity of informing or involving the child's parents or any other person. In this way, it is possible to obtain the court order very quickly indeed.

The order lasts for eight days only and can be extended for a further seven days. After 72 hours, an application for its discharge can be made.

The child assessment order

This order is a new concept, the above replacing orders already in existence. Although a local authority may feel that a child is at risk there are times when it cannot gain access to the child to compile evidence. In the past the local authority could apply for a place of safety order and remove the child immediately from its home. It could also do nothing.

The child assessment order has effect for seven days maximum. With such an order it is possible to remove a child from its home. There is no parental responsibility. The intention behind the order is to enable the local authority to assess the child so it can make the necessary arrangements after consideration.

Before the Children's Act came into being, it was possible to make orders giving a local authority the right to intervene in a child's life under a number of jurisdictions, some overlapping. The Children's Act is now the only jurisdiction under which a local authority may act. By section 31 (4) an application for a care order or a supervision order can be made on its own or within family proceedings as defined by section 8 (3) of the Act. Applications for education supervision orders, emergency protection orders and child assessment orders have to made alone.

Categories of applicants for orders are limited:

Care orders, supervision orders and child assessment orders-only a local authority or NSPCC may apply

Education supervision orders-only a local education authority may apply.

Emergency protection orders-only a local authority may apply.

In place of previous powers to make different orders, the court now has intermediate powers under section 37. Where a court is dealing with family proceedings in which a question relating to the welfare of a child arises, it may direct the local authority to carry out investigations. The local authority must respond and decide what order should be applied for. If the local authority decides not to apply for an order the court cannot make it do so, although this fact must be reported to the court.

Grounds on which a court will grant an order (s 31(2))

A court has to be satisfied of the following before granting an order:

a) that the child has suffered or is likely to suffer significant harm

b) that the harm or likelihood of harm is attributable to the care given to the child, or likely to be given to him if the order were not made or the child being beyond parental control.

Proof of the ground in section 31(2) only entitles court to grant a care or supervision order. The court does not have to grant such an order. The grounds in this section are referred to as "threshold" grounds.

In relation to education and supervision orders, the court has to be satisfied that the child is of compulsory school age and not being properly educated.

To obtain an emergency protection order, the local authority must demonstrate the following:

a) a local authority must show that the enquiries are being frustrated and that access to the child is required urgently

b) the NSPCC must show that it has reasonable cause to suspect that the child is in danger of suffering significant harm

c) any other applicant must show that there is reasonable cause to believe that the child is likely to suffer significant harm if he is not removed from the home.

As with the other orders, applications for emergency protection orders are subject to section 1 of the Act.

For child assessment orders, the court has to be satisfied that:

a) the applicant has reasonable cause to suspect that the child is suffering or likely to suffer significant harm

b) this can only be determined by an assessment of the child's health or development

c) it is not likely that an assessment can be made without an order.

Again, applications for this order are subject to section 1 of the Children Act.

Parental contact

By section 34 of the Act a local authority is under a duty to allow reasonable contact between a child in care and his parents. If there is any dispute on the reasonableness of contact, the court can regulate. In limited circumstances, a local authority can refuse to allow contact for up to seven days.

By section 43, if a child is to be kept away from home during the currency of the child assessment order, the order must contain directions for such contact between the child and other persons as the court thinks fit.

By section 44, an applicant who is granted such an order is placed under a duty to allow reasonable contact between child and parents.

Wardship

Wardship is the means by which the family court fulfils its jurisdiction of protection of children. When a child becomes a ward of court, the court controls its upbringing by a series of directions and orders. Wardship does not only deal with issues of where and with whom the child lives but also with other important issues, for example consenting to medical treatment or other issues. The flexibility of wardship appeals to local authorities who often go down this route in preference to care proceedings

However, by section 100 of the Children's Act, no local authority may apply to make a child a ward of court unless it has leave of the court to do so. These grounds are very limited and wardship is, on the face of it, used in very limited circumstances.

CHAPTER NINE

THE FAMILY LAW ACT 1996

Background to the Act

The Family Law Act 1996 received the Royal Assent on 4th July 1996. Parts 1,2 and 3 deal with the reform of the law of divorce and other related matters. Because of the complexity of the legislation and the controversy that has accompanied it, these sections of the Act are not likely to come into force for another 2-3 years. The purpose of this chapter is to outline the proposed new changes which will radically change the law and procedure for divorce when eventually they come into force.

The provisions of Part 4 of the Act were originally contained in separate legislation, the Family Homes and Domestic Violence Bill, which was withdrawn in late October 1995 following objections from a substantial number of MP's.

It is expected that Part IV dealing with the occupation of the family home, the prevention of molestation and other related matters will come into effect in October 1997.

The Family Law Bill itself was introduced into the House of Commons on 16th November 1995 and continued on its way, with amendments, to Royal Assent.
By way of background, the debate concerning divorce and the need for reform has been going on for some years now and in 1988, the Law Commission issued a discussion paper "Facing the future A discussion

paper on the Ground for divorce" (Law Com no 170). In this paper the law commission acknowledged that there were concerns as to the effectiveness of the present divorce law set out in the Matrimonial Causes Act 1973. Although the sole ground for divorce was that the marriage had irretrievably broken down, for a divorce to be obtained quickly, adultery or unreasonable behaviour had to be alleged and it was felt that this led to acrimony and bitterness between the parties and had an adverse effect on children. In consequence, opportunities for reconciliation were lost and many marriages which might have been saved were dissolved.

The alternative basis for divorce, relying on two years separation with the consent of the respondent, was frequently not available to partners on lower incomes because separation may be impossible without substantial resources-hence the law was discriminatory in its operation.

The Law Commission concluded by stating that reform was urgently needed and offering alternative divorce models. The discussion paper was followed by the Law Commission's 1990 Report "Family Law-the Ground for Divorce" (Law Com No 192). The Report repeated the criticisms of the present law.

After analysing several models, the Law Commission recommended that irretrievable breakdown of marriage should remain the sole ground for divorce and that divorce should no longer be seen as a single event but should rather be a process over time culminating in a divorce order. This would provide parties with an opportunity to determine whether the marriage had in fact broken down irretrievably, to face up to the consequences of divorce and to make practical arrangements for the future.

The government responded to the Law Commission by issuing its own consultation paper in December 1993 "Looking To The Future: Mediation and The Ground For Divorce". The government had made mediation one of the central planks of its consultation paper, in contrast to the Law Commission. This was further reinforced in its subsequent White Paper "Looking To The Future: Mediation and The Ground for Divorce" (CM 2799) published in April 1995.

The governments principal recommendation for reform was as follows:

" The government proposes...that it should be possible to obtain a divorce in England and Wales on the sole ground that the marriage has irretrievably broken down. The breakdown of the marriage should be demonstrated by the passing of a period of time for reflection and consideration in order for the couple to address what has gone wrong in the marriage, whether there is any hope of reconciliation and in the event that the breakdown is irretrievable, to make proper arrangements for living apart once a divorce order is made. The government proposed that the minimum period for reflection and consideration should be twelve months".

Reform of the law relating to domestic violence and occupation of the family home

Following the publication 1n 1989 of a working paper "Domestic Violence and Occupation of the Family Home (Working Paper no 113) the Law Commission reviewed the present state of the law in its 1992 report "Family Law: Domestic Violence and Occupation of the Family Home" (Law Com No 207).

It identified a number of anomalies and inconsistencies stemming principally from the fact that different courts offer different remedies applying different criteria. The Law Commission advocated that all courts should have the same jurisdiction to make non molestation orders and occupation orders, that each order should have its own criteria but the orders should be capable of combination with each other and with other family remedies in appropriate cases. It also recommended that a wider range of applicants should be able to seek orders from the court. It introduced the concept of "associated persons" and recommended the retention of ex parte orders and the improvement in methods of enforcement with the court being required to attach a power of arrest in certain circumstances rather than having the discretion to do so as is the case under present law.

Further, it recommended that the power to transfer tenancies, at present contained in the Matrimonial Homes Act 1983 , should be extended to cohabitants and it proposed changes to the powers of the courts in making emergency protection orders under s 44 of the Children Act 1989.

In the next chapter we will be looking at the principles of Parts 2 and 3 of the Act as set out in part 1 (s1) . These sections cover proposed changes to the divorce law.

CHAPTER TEN

PRINCIPLES OF THE ACT

The general principles governing the operation of Parts 2 and 3 of the Family Law Act are set out in part 1(s.1) and they represent that framework within which the court and all others who use the Act must operate. They are that:

a) the institution of marriage is to be supported;

b) the parties to a marriage which may have broken down are to be encouraged to take all practicable steps, whether by marriage counselling or otherwise, to save the marriage;

c) a marriage which has irretrievably broken down and is being brought to an end should be brought to an end-

i) with the minimum distress to the parties and to the children affected;

ii) with questions dealt with in a manner designed to promote as good a continuing relationship between the parties and any children affected as is possible in the circumstances ;

iii) without costs being reasonably incurred in connection with the procedures to be followed in bringing it to an end;

d) that any risk to one of the parties to a marriage, and to any children, of violence from the other party should, so far as is reasonably practicable, be removed or diminished.

The general principles do not, however, govern the operation of Part 4 of the Act which deals with domestic violence. The Lord Chancellor saw the provisions of Part 4 as being quite separate from those in Parts 1, 2 and 3.

The Procedure for separation and divorce

As stated the ground for divorce in the Family Law Act 1996 is the irretrievable breakdown of the marriage as demonstrated by the sole fact of a period for reflection and consideration. (s. 5(1)).

A marriage will only be taken to have broken down irretrievably if:

a) a statement has been made by one or both of the parties that the maker of the statement believes that the marriage has broken down;

b) the statement complies with the requirements of s 6 of the Act

c) the period for reflection and consideration has ended:

d) the application for a separation and divorce order under s 3 is accompanied by a declaration by the party making the application that-

i) having reflected on the breakdown, and

ii) having considered the requirements of Part 2 of the Act as to the parties arrangements for the future, the applicant believes that the marriage cannot be saved.

The statement and the application for a separation or divorce order do not have to be made by the same party (s. 5(2)). No application for a separation or divorce order can be made with reference to a particular statement if:

a) the parties have jointly given notice withdrawing the statement;

b) the period of one year (specified period) has passed since the end of the period for reflection and consideration (s 5(3)(b).

There are several steps to be taken towards the divorce order, which differentiates the new law from old:

a) one or both of the parties must attend an information meeting. They are encouraged to attend marriage counselling;

b) at least three months later, a statement of marital breakdown is lodged with the court, and served by the court on the other party (unless it has been made jointly)

c) the period for reflection and consideration commences fourteen days after the statement has been lodged with the court. This will last for a minimum of 9 months. It may be extended by one further period of 6 months in certain circumstances.

d) the parties may formally notify the court that they wish to "stop the clock" in relation to the period of reflection and consideration in order to start reconciliation. If the period is extended for more than 18 months, then a new statement must be lodged before an application for a separation of divorce order can be made.

e) when the period for reflection and consideration expires, either or both parties may apply to the court for a separation or divorce order. The statement will lapse if an application for an order is not made within 1 year of the end of the period for reflection and consideration (unless the lapse period has been extended)

f) a divorce or separation order will only be granted if the court is satisfied as to the parties arrangements for the future.

g) an order preventing divorce may be made in certain circumstances.

The Act provides that it will not be possible to commence the process which would lead to divorce, within the first year of marriage, nor will it be possible for a separation order which is made before the second anniversary of the marriage to be converted into a divorce order until after the second anniversary.

It is possible to commence the process for a separation order within the first year of marriage. It cannot however, be granted until after one year has elapsed. A person wishing to initiate proceedings for separation or divorce must first attend a compulsory information meeting before the period of time starts to run which might lead to divorce. Having attended this meeting the party initiating the separation or divorce must wait for a cooling off period of 3 months before lodging with the court a statement of marital breakdown.

The receipt of the statement by the court starts the clock running for the nine months period of reflection or consideration. The divorce can be obtained following this period. If there is a child in the family who is under 16 s. 7(11) and 7(13) provides that the period of reflection and consideration is automatically extended by six months, unless the conditions in s. 7 (12) satisfy the court that the divorce should not be delayed.

If one, or both, of the parties wish for further time to consider their future arrangements then they may apply for the period of reflection and consideration to be extended by six months. The court will not allow an extension if (s. 7(12)):

a) at the time when an application for the divorce order is made, there is an occupation order or a non molestation order in force in favour of the applicant, or of a child of the family, made against the other party.

b) the court is satisfied that delaying the making of a divorce order would be significantly detrimental to the welfare of any child of the family.

Separation and divorce orders

Under the new system established by the Act, the court may make:

a) a divorce order-which dissolves a marriage (s. 2(1)(a)

b) a separation order-which provides for the separation of the parties to a marriage (s. 2(1)(b)

The court will only make either of the above orders if it is satisfied that the following conditions are made:

a) the marriage has broken down irretrievably ;

b) the requirements of s.8 in relation to information meetings have been met:

c) the requirements of s. 9 in relation to the parties arrangements for the future have been met;

d) the application has not been withdrawn. No order for divorce can be made if there is an order preventing divorce by virtue of the "hardship bar". This is within s. 10, the Act giving the court power to postpone or bar altogether a divorce where one party can show that dissolution of the marriage would result in substantial or other hardship The bar is available in all cases.

As was outlined earlier, great emphasis is put on attendance at information meetings prior to any order being granted. At these meetings, details of which are still being firmed up, stress will be given to attendance at mediation meetings and marriage counselling. The initial period of reflection therefore carries with it much importance within the new legislative framework. To underpin this, the Lord Chancellor has taken over financial responsibility for the setting up of marriage support services. Grants will be provided, along with grants for research into the causes of marital breakdown and prevention of such.

Marriage support services will cover all aspects of marriage, from couples thinking of divorcing to those thinking of getting married. The aim is to provide a thoroughly professional service which will serve alongside the new legislation.

CHAPTER ELEVEN

FINANCIAL PROVISION UNDER THE ACT

The main source of law on financial provision and property adjustment remains part 2 of the Matrimonial Causes Act 1973, as amended most recently by s. 166 of the Pensions Act 1995 and Schedules 2 and 8 of the 1996 Act.

Section 15 of the 1996 Act confirms that schedule 2 amends the 1973 Act and provides:

The main object of schedule 2 is-

a) to provide that, in the case of divorce or separation, an order about financial provision may be made under that Act before a divorce or separation order is made; but

b) to retain (with minor changes) the position under that Act where marriages are annulled.

Financial provision and property adjustment orders

Schedule 2 of the FLA 1996 amends part 2 of the Matrimonial Causes Act 1973. Section 21 of the 1973 Act is substituted by sch 2 para 2 (1) of the Act and principally contains relevant definitions.

The FLA will substitute and amend many clauses in the 1973 Act in relation to financial and property orders and this will become clearer when the legislation comes into force. There will be amendments to the courts powers to vary orders also.

CHAPTER TWELVE

ASSOCIATED PERSONS OR RELEVANT CHILD

As will be seen, in determining whether a client will be able to obtain a non molestation order under the Family Law Act 1996 the first matter to be ascertained is whether the applicant and respondent are "associated" within the meaning of the Act or, where the person sought to be protected is a child, whether the child is a "relevant "child.

The list of associated persons appears in s. 62 (4) and (5) of the Act and covers persons who, prior to the 1996 Act could not obtain injunctive relief unless they were able to rely upon behaviour which was capable of amounting to a tort or threatened tort and so bring a civil action to which injunctive relief might attach.

Persons are associated with each other if:

a) they are married

b) they have been married

c) they are cohabitants

d) they are former cohabitants

e) they live in the same household

f) they have lived in the same household

g) they are relatives

h) they have agreed to marry each other

I) they are parents of the same child

j) they have, or have had, parental responsibility for the same child

k) they are parties to the same family proceedings. The exception to this is where one of the parties is a body corporate (local authority).

There are exclusions from the above list. There was some discussion on certain categories of people living together. However, the Lord Chancellor was mindful not to exclude homosexual couples who can also apply for a non molestation order.

Matrimonial Home Rights

The Family Law Act largely reproduces the provisions of the Matrimonial Homes Act 1983, referred to earlier. However, it also resolves a problem namely that the MHA gave no powers to make orders in respect of a property which the parties intended to be their home but in which they never actually lived together. The situation will be that the court will have power to make orders in respect of any dwelling house which is, or is intended to be, the joint home of the parties.

Apart from this, modifications to the Matrimonial Homes Act are minimal, with the exception of changes in terminology to ensure consistency with various Housing Acts.

Matrimonial Home Rights under the 1996 Act

Where one spouse is entitled to occupy a dwelling house by virtue of a beneficial estate or contract and the other spouse is not entitled, s. 30 of the 1996 Act gives the non entitled spouse matrimonial home rights. Those rights are:

a) if in occupation, a right not to be evicted or excluded form the dwelling house or any part of it by the other spouse except with leave of the court, given by order under s. 33;

b) if not in occupation, a right a with the leave of the court to enter into and occupy the dwelling house.

If a spouse has an equitable, rather than a legal, interest in the home, s. 30(9) provides that she has the same matrimonial home rights as a spouse with no interest whatsoever in it.

Security of tenure

Occupation by the spouse with matrimonial home rights is, by virtue of s. 30 (4) treated as occupation by the other spouse for the purposes of the Rent (Agriculture) Act 1976, the Rent Act 1977 and the Housing Acts. This provision may help the wife stave off possession proceedings, but her matrimonial home rights are against her husband, rather than his landlord. Applications can be made for transfer of a tenancy which is dealt with further on.

Occupation orders

The Family Law Act attempts to simplify matters by granting courts the power to make a single order in relation to the home. The order is known as an occupation order. There is a distinction drawn between what are known as "non entitled applicants" and "entitled" applicants. Entitled applicants have a legal or beneficial interest in the home, non entitled applicants do not. Non entitled applicants can only apply for orders against former spouses, cohabitants or former cohabitants.

Application can be made under five different sections of Part 1V of the Act for an occupation order. To decide which section is applicable in a particular case the status of the applicant and respondent must be determined. The scheme of the Act favours married couples and property owners by offering them a greater level of protection.

Ancillary orders-the courts powers

Section 40(1)(a) of the Act provides that the court may, on making an order under ss 33, 35 or 36-or at any time thereafter-impose on either party obligations as to:

the repair and maintenance of the dwelling house
the discharge of rent
the discharge of mortgage payments
the discharge of other outgoings affecting the dwelling house.

It is anticipated that this power will be particularly useful when an occupation order continues for some time or while the outcome of the proceedings under the Matrimonial Causes Act 1973 is awaited.

The Law Commission also suggested that the court should have power to order an occupying party to make payments to the other for that occupation. Under the old law only the non entitled spouse could be ordered to make such payments.

The courts powers

In deciding whether, and if so, how to exercise its powers the court must have regard to all the circumstances of the case, including:

a) the financial needs and financial resources of the parties:

b) the financial obligations which they have or are likely to have in the foreseeable future to each other and to any relevant child.

CHAPTER THIRTEEN

NON MOLESTATION ORDERS

As we have discussed, a non molestation order is an order which prevents one person from molesting another. For the purposes of the Family Law Act it is relevant to associated persons.

Section 42 (2) allows the court to make a non molestation order in the following circumstances:

a) if an application has been made by a person who is associated with the respondent:

i) in other family proceedings

ii) in the absence of any other family proceedings

b) without an application being made:

i) in any family proceedings to which the respondent is already a party

ii) if the court considers that the order should be made for the benefit of any other party to the proceedings or to any relevant child.

Whether or not a non molestation order is made lies within the discretion of the court. In exercising its discretion the court has to have regard to all the circumstances including the need to secure the health and safety and well being of the applicant, the other party to the proceedings or the relevant child. This test places less emphasis than the previous law on the violence of the respondent. The courts can make orders for any specified period.

Ex Parte orders and undertakings

Section 45 of the Act preserves the power of the court to grant non molestation orders and occupation orders ex parte. The overriding principle is that the court should only exercise its discretion in this area where it is just and convenient to do so.

The Child as applicant

Under the 1996 Act, a child under the age of 16 may not apply for an occupation order or a non molestation order without the leave of the court. Leave will only be granted if the court is satisfied that the child has *sufficient understanding* to make the proposed application. As we discussed earlier, the issue of the sufficiency of a child's understanding was considered by the House of Lords in Gillick v West Norfolk and Wisbech Area Health Authority and another (1986). It was held that the parental right to decide whether or not medical treatment could be given to a child under 16 terminated if and when the child achieved a sufficient understanding to enable her to fully understand what was proposed.

Enforcement of orders

The Domestic Violence and Matrimonial Proceedings Act 1976 permitted the High Court and the County court to attach a power of arrest to an injunction containing an exclusion order or restraining one party from using violence. The Domestic Violence and Matrimonial Proceedings Act 1978 allowed magistrates to attach powers of arrest in broadly similar circumstances. However, under the above legislation, the High courts and the County courts did not sharer the power of magistrates to issue arrest warrants or to remand a person arrested pursuant to a power of arrest pending proceedings being taken for breach of an order.

The 1996 Act extends the powers of the High court and County Courts to bring them in line with those already enjoyed by the magistrates court.

CHAPTER FOURTEEN

TRANSFER OF TENANCIES

The Matrimonial Homes Act 1983 allowed the court 'on decree...or at any time thereafter' to transfer certain tenancies between spouses or former spouses. No power, however, existed to transfer tenancies between co-habitees. Therefore, a key amendment has been made.

Under the 1996 act where one cohabitant is entitled (either in his own right or jointly with the other cohabitants) to occupy a dwelling house by virtue of a relevant tenancy (protected or statutory), governed by the 1977 Rent Act, statutory tenancy within the meaning of the Rent (Agriculture) Act 1976, Secure tenancy governed by the 1985 Housing Act or assured tenancy governed by the 1988 Housing Act) and the cohabitants cease to live together as husband and wife, sch 7, para 3 permits the court to make an order at any time after they cease to live together.

Under sch 7 para 4 the court can only make an order if the dwelling house is or was:

a) in the case of spouses, a matrimonial home;

b) in the case of cohabitants, a home in which they lived together as husband and wife.

Part Two Orders

Protected, secure or assured tenancy or assured agricultural occupancy-

Schedule 7, para 7 provides that the court may by order direct that from a specified date the estate or interest of one spouse or cohabitant be transferred to and vested in the other spouse or cohabitant.

Additional provisions

The protection of children

The 1996 Act has amended the 1989 Children Act to give the court power to make short term, emergency ouster orders for the benefit of children. The power is intended to be a supplement to an emergency protection order or an interim care order, rather than an alternative. Instead of using the word "ouster" the Act has created the term "exclusion requirement"

CONCLUSION

It is hoped that this book has helped the reader through the maze of family law.

Legislation in this area is fast changing and the 1996 Family Law Act will give practitioners and students plenty of food for thought for the foreseeable future.

Those people who experience the trauma of a breakup of the family are the very people which the law seeks to protect, and also to impose obligations. Children are quite often the passive recipients of separation and divorce, or of battles over parenthood. It is because the whole area of family law is so complex that it is continuously evolving.

The next few years heralds a complete change in the law concerning divorce and it is hoped (by myself) that it makes life easier for those who use it. Ultimately, there is no easy answer to human relationships and it requires great skill on the part of those who dispense professional advice and strength on the part of those caught up in trauma in order to arrive at a clear settlement, a settlement which benefits adults and children in the future.

This book is but a brief overview of the law and I hope that it will provide the foundation for a more in depth study.

USEFUL ADDRESSES

The Child Support Agency
PO Box 55
brierley Hill
West Midlands DY5 1YL.

Tel: 01345 133133.

Courts Family Division
Principal Registry
Somerset House
Strand
London WC2R 1LP

Law Centres Federation
Duchess House
18-19 Warren Street
London W1P 5DB.

Tel: 0171 387 8570.

The Law Society
113 Chancery Lane
London WC2A 1PL.

Tel: 0171 242 1222.

Legal Aid Board
29-37 Red Lion Street
London WC1R 4PP.

Tel: 0171 831 4209.

The Family Law Bar Association
Queen Elizabeth Building
Temple
London EC4Y 9BS.

Tel: 0171 797 7837.

Family Mediators Association
The Old House
Rectory Gardens
Henbury
Bristol BS10 7AQ.

Tel: 01272 500140.

Family Policies Study Centre
231 Baker Street
London NW1 6XE.

Tel: 0171 486 8211.

Family Rights Group
The Print House
18 Ashwin Street
London E8 3DL

Tel: 0171 923 2628.

Family Service Units
207 Marylebone Road
London NW1 5QP.

Gingerbread (Guidance for single parents and Children)
35 Wellington Street
London WC2E 7BN.

Tel: 0171 240 0953.

Head of Family Law Division
Lord Chancellors Department
Southside
105 Victoria Street
London SW1E 6QT.

Tel: 0171 210 2059.

The National Council for one parent families
255 Kentish Town Road
London NW5 2LX.

Tel: 0171 267 1361.

The National Family Conciliation Council
Shaftesbury Centre
Percy Street
Swindon
Wiltshire
SN2 2AZ.

Tel: 01793 514055

National Organisation for the Counselling of Adoptees and Parents.
3 New High Street
Headington
Oxford OX3 7AJ.

Tel: 01865 750554

National Stepfamily Association
72 Willesden Lane
London NW6 7TA.

Tel: 0171 372 0844.

Relate Marriage Guidance
Herbert Gray College
Little Church Street
Rugby
Warwickshire CV21 3AP.

Tel: 01788 573241.

INDEX

T

V

W

OTHER GUIDES IN THIS SERIES

Other guides in the series are:

Easyway Guides:

Guide to Letting Property
Guide to Bankruptcy and Insolvency
Guide to Buying and Selling a Home
Guide to Writing a C.V and passing interviews
Guide to Employment Law
Guide to Small Claims
Guide to Consumer Law

If you would like to comment on this book or produce a guide for the series please write to:

Easyway Guides
38 Cromwell Rd
London E17 9JN